Sufficiently Educated

From struggling to a college

degree

An autobiography about

learning disabilities in

education

By Jeremiah O'Neal

Sufficiently Educated

From struggling to a college degree

An autobiography about learning disabilities in

education

Library of Congress Control Number:

2020917663

ISBN# 978-0-578-75560-1

Pricetag: $9.00

Contents

Prologue

Thank you for taking the time to read the first edition of my book. When you have the time, please visit my website at http://SufficientlyEducated.com and fill out the questionnaire QK:b9192020k. I decided to write this book because of what was going on at the beginning of the election year. I wanted to provide a resource that students going through primary and secondary school could use to help them on the way through their education and to hopefully achieve their first or second degree at the end. There are a lot of great books that are available to help students that need tips on how to study and how to prepare for college. This is not one of those books. Instead, this is a book about my life and what I went through from the beginning up to the point where I received my bachelor's degree. I'm also not bringing up everything in my life, only the stories that are unique to me and would serve to help others. I hope you enjoy this book.

Chapter 1 - Introduction

Five years ago if you had asked me to write this book, I would have said *no*. However, after what I saw in the last election between Donald Trump and Hillary Clinton, something eventually clicked in my mind. I can remember the image of Mr. Trump mocking the reporter, Mr. Kovaleski, not for his report but for his disability. Seeing this concerned me because a respectable, highly intelligent person can have their dignity squelched by a man like Mr. Trump just because they are different. Therefore, my goal in writing this book is to create a road map that others can follow based on how my life began and how I've achieved educational success from primary school to college. Throughout the writing of this book, I've drawn inspiration from several other books written by people with disabilities.

In a book written by Sam Sagmiller, entitled *Dyslexia My Life*, Mr. Sagmiller writes about an incident that happened to him in school. He describes a scene where a student teacher was assigned to his study group to help him and the other students. At one point, the student teacher became enraged. Instead of helping the students, the student teacher picked up a pair of scissors and nearly stabbed Mr. Sagmiller through the hand. Reading this really upset me, but then I recalled a time in first grade when my teacher placed soap in my mouth for something that I said. So I realize that at any time, children, especially those with disabilities, are vulnerable to abuse. It is just that some of us try to hide that abuse and forget about it. The good news is after my first-grade teacher told my mother that she had put soap in my mouth, I was immediately taken out of that school. However, I am very sorry for the students who cannot get out of these terrible situations.

In order to strengthen the disabled community, students with disabilities need to start advancing toward their educational objectives and think past the past stigmas associated with being disabled. According to a BLS graph in 2014, 16.4% of disabled adults aged twenty-four and older have a bachelor's degree, while 34.6% of nondisabled adults have a bachelor's degree. One nondisabled adult in five has a high school diploma, while one disabled adult in ten has a high school diploma. (People with disabilities are less likely to have completed a bachelor's degree, (people with a disability less likely to have completed a bachelors degree 2019). "Underemployment" is the term that defines someone who is employed in a position that does not fully utilize their skills. BLS reported in 2019 that 31.1% of disabled employees worked at the management level, while 41.1% of nondisabled employees worked at the management level. On the other hand, 20.7% of disabled employees worked in service occupations, while 17.0% of nondisabled employees also worked in service occupations. (Persons with a Disability: Labor Force Characteristics Summary 2019). In the 2018 voter turnout on census.gov, the report tells us that 27.2% of adults without high school diplomas voted, whereas 65.7% of adults with bachelor's degrees voted (census.gov 2019). These factors show a link between disabled adults who voted and nondisabled adults who voted based on the fact that non-college-educated adults are less likely to vote and that disabled adults are less likely to have a degree, which would be a requirement to work at the management level.

A lot of the protections that help disabled children depend on policymaking. One such act is the IDEA act. The Individuals with Disabilities Education Act was established in 1990 to replace EHA. The IDEA made significant changes to support students with disabilities. These changes focused more on the individual than the disability. If, for example, two students had an auditory processing disorder, each student would receive an IEP with their own plans and goals. As of 2006, more than six million children in the United States receive special education services through IDEA (Individuals with Disabilities Education Act 2019). This is why it's important that people with disabilities have a voice in politics starting with votes that matter: these acts play a significant part in helping children who are part of the disabled demographic.

When you start to look at some of the problems that we're facing today, most have to do with the damaging decisions being made by President Trump. "The Trump administration's fiscal year 2020 budget would make cuts across multiple agencies and offices that serve Americans with disabilities, stripping them of essential resources." (Trump's Budget Is Full of Cuts Aimed at People With Disabilities 2019). These decisions are problematic for the disabled who need these services the most. Unless someone speaks for the disabled and votes for people that can put a stop to these disastrous decisions, disabled people will continue to lose much-needed services.

So the question remains: how do we reverse these policies crippling our disabled population? Either the nondisabled population needs to start voting for politicians that will change the laws to favor the disabled, or the disabled population needs to rise up and advance themselves to a level where they can make voting decisions on their own. These are only a few ideas that come to mind when I think about this problem. But these are also solutions that need to be enacted right now if we're to see equality among disabled and nondisabled people in the United States.

In an effort to help, in this book I write about my life from birth to the time I finished college. The idea behind this book is to share encounters I've had throughout my life. These are not meant to make anyone's life better but rather inspirational stories of my journey to where I am today. While I will not be revealing every minute detail of my life, I will bring up some of the more interesting characteristics and also some of the encounters that I had. One of the most critical parts of what made me who I am is that I am incredibly goal oriented. If there's something that I want, I will pursue it. I think that this is one of the hallmarks of my success and what really drove me to completing my education and entering my chosen career field.

Chapter 2 – Elementary / Middle School

I came into the world on March 24 at 10:58 p.m. at the University of California Medical, San Diego. My half-sister, Kerrie O'Neal, was a talented musician and would later spend much of her time with me on the piano. She must have inherited her talent from my father, who enjoyed playing the guitar and would have competitions with my uncle, Curt, to see who was the best musician in the family. My paternal grandfather, Lester, was born in New Castle, Lawrence, PA, by John and Alice. John's parents, Edward McCabe and Sarah Ann McCabe (McAvoy), immigrated from Scotland and Ireland in 1884. My great grandfather, John McCabe, had a very difficult life when his parents died and was placed in an orphanage. The orphanage was a really bad place for John and his brother and sister. He was treated horribly by the nuns. Early in my life, my mother and father separated, making things very difficult for my mother. However, both my mother's and father's parents (Alfred—my father's stepfather, Noma—my father's mother, Robert—my mother's father, and Betty—my mother's mother) were very supportive. After the separation, things became a lot better for my mother and me. My maternal grandfather, Robert, would take me on exciting trips across California and Arizona including to Sequoia National Park and the Grand Canyon. My mother's parents, their parents, and her sister's family were always having get togethers. Eventually, my uncle would introduce me to his personal computer and the game Zork by Infocom.

Zork is a text adventure game developed in the 1980s by staff and students at the Massachusetts Institute of Technology under the aegis of the software company named Infocom. Zork uses an interpreter called the Z-Machine that takes commands from the user and deciphers what the user would like to do. For example, if there was a lamp and the user wanted to turn on the lamp, then a command that the user could try would be *get lamp*. This verb and noun combination was just enough to allow the game to understand what the user wanted to do. In addition to a lot of typing, there was a lot of reading. "An epicene gnome of zurich wearing a three-piece suit and carrying a safety-deposit box materialized in the room." (Zork 2019)

My uncle showed me Zork on his PC. Everything was controlled by the keyboard using a combination of noun and verb commands to perform actions. My uncle started the game by selecting Zork from a text menu. As he did this, I could hear the hard drive spin as the game loaded. Then the screen lit up with paragraphs of text. This included a description of who made Zork and what needed to be done first to progress through the game. The first task was to open the mailbox and read what was inside. The game was devoid of any graphics, and there wasn't a narrator doing the reading (rather the person playing the game was the one reading). If I wanted to know what was going on around me, I would have to type *look*, and the game would show a line of text describing what was going on. I would ask my uncle all the time about what words meant and what I could do to advance in the game. It took me quite a while to figure out what some of the text even meant.

In addition to reading and typing, there were also a lot of puzzle elements in the game. It's not like a "pick your own action" in order to progress to the next page. There were times when things had to be done in a certain order to get to the next part. An example of this was in the maze section. There was a lot of outside-the-box thinking and creativity to get past this part. The convenience of a built-in map or a journal was not part of the game, and any mapmaking or note taking had to be done by hand. My uncle had pages of maps on each section of the game. After a while, I eventually leaned how to get into the house and get the lamp, which would be one of the key items needed to progress through the rest of the game. All of this took some time, looking over clues and asking my uncle for help, but I was still learning and somewhere between elementary and middle school, I had advanced through almost 90% of the game.

I've never felt like I really wanted to learn how to read and write before until I started playing Zork. There was an incentive that by understanding what was going on, I could progress and find out what would happen next. Zork was like the simple form of a book, but there was also the challenge of needing to know what each word meant. The option to skip the difficult words was no longer there for me. I had to understand every word in order to understand what was going on and what I needed to do to make my next decision. In addition to that, I had to learn to write words. Once I understood the simple commands like the cardinal directions, those commands could easily be repeated; so in that sense, learning the commands was not that difficult. But it still took time to learn the commands in the first place and then to repeat the commands again. That's why when my uncle gave me the commands once, he expected me to remember them. Overall, this game played a huge part in my development. I was strengthening not only my vocabulary but also my memorization skills.

Chapter 2.1 – Personal Interests

In third grade, I developed an interest in a line of toys called "spy-tech." Each spy-tech toy set included everything needed to perform a spy activity. Some of the spy-tech kits included a camera with a mirror that could be used to take pictures around corners and also a fingerprint dusting kit (Toys of the eighties, Spy Tech 2019). I was quite preoccupied by my new hobby, decoding messages and learning Morse Code. My third-grade elementary teacher knew about my spy-tech hobby and my interest in becoming a spy.

She met with me one day, and I explained that I wanted to demonstrate one of the activities in the spy-tech kit with the class. I showed my teacher the spy-tech fingerprinting kit and explained how it worked. The kit came with everything that was needed to both take and lift fingerprints. This kit included cards and an ink pad for taking and pressing prints. In addition, the kit came with a brush, powder, and inverted black cards for taking the prints off an object.

Before the day when I would demonstrate my hobby to the class, five students were selected to help me demonstrate. In another classroom, I rolled each of the students' fingers on the ink pad and then onto one of the index cards. Each student had one of several fingerprint patterns. Different patterns were used to match the print. On the day that I presented my hobby to the class, one of the five students pressed their fingers against a flat object. It was then my job to figure out who touched the object. Using the powder, brush, tape, and inverted black cards, I began to brush the powder onto the object. After a while, the print began to appear, and I took it off the object using the tape and placed the tape onto the black card. The white powder on the tape and the black card gave me a clear image of the print. At that moment, I began to go over each of the index cards that I took from the previous day with the student's fingerprints on them and began comparing the lifted print to the fingerprint index cards. I remember that I was staring at each card one by one, looking at the details of the print for anything close to a match. After some time, I stood up and stared at the students. I had an idea of whose print matched the print that I lifted, but I was not absolutely sure. One of the students giggled, and by chance I named this student as my suspect. Sure enough, I was correct in my identification. My interest in spy tech would last a little longer. I had an interest in investigating things and dreamed of one day working for the FBI.

I always had a deep desire to learn about the mechanical operations of devices and how they functioned. Figuring out how electrical and mechanical devices work is something that has stayed with me for a very long time. I remember looking at the ceiling and following the wires to their destination or to where they connected to, curious to know why they were there and what they did. I was interested in the systems and how things operated. Even today, I enjoy looking at the inner workings of something and seeing what makes it perform its task.

As a young child, I would learn how to take things apart, especially when it came to my electronic toys. I always wanted to know what made the wheels turn. I'd follow the wheels to a bunch of gears that were all connected to a motor. I don't think I got the concept of what the motor did at that time, but I was curious as to why the wheels turned. Later on in my childhood, I would build little circuits that would do things, including a simple alarm system that would let me know if someone came in before me. I enjoyed working with my hands as a child. I especially enjoyed doing outside projects. One day, I asked my mother if we could build a 2½-foot deep oval-shaped pond in the backyard. Using concrete and some other materials, we turned the lake and stream that I dug into a pond with a small waterfall and a pump. Then we added some fish. Something about seeing these little projects becoming permanent gave me a sense of accomplishment. I could observe the entire scope of the project I was working on from the moment it was just an idea to when it became a fully working system containing a waterfall, pump, and fish. From that point forward, I would sit by the pond listening to the splash of the water as it traveled over the falls while watching the fish swim about.

One day, my grandmother bought an electronic Casio piano, and every week I would visit her and explore my creative musical skills. I didn't know what I was doing, but through trial and error I was able to create something with a melodic feel. The process of creating the melody and hearing the playback of that creation felt amazing to me. I was always setting out little milestones from where I left off. That is why I felt that the projects were so significant to me: I was experiencing the process from start to finish. I enjoyed doing the things like pressing a key, hearing a tone, and then pressing multiple keys and hearing a melody. To me, it was a feeling of expression in another language that only I could make sense of.

Chapter 2.2 – Faith and Learning

Before I was old enough to go to Sunday school at the Lutheran church, I would sit with my grandfather in the pew. I didn't really understand what the pastor was talking about; so instead, I would resort to doodling on some scrap paper on the back of the pew next to the bibles. I'd also watch the organ player as he played the notes. I was mostly interested in the buttons he was pushing. An assortment of different knobs and push buttons were scattered all over the organ as he would push and turn them, producing the sounds in the church. Eventually, I would become old enough to go to Sunday school. During that time, I remember doing arts-and-crafts projects, and later on I would rehearse a line out of the Bible that I would later read to all of the parents in the church.

In addition to going to church, I was also taking swimming classes at a public pool. My grandparents had a pool that I used to wade in and the swimming class that I took would help me learn how to swim around my grandparents' pool with more confidence. The swimming class at the public pool helped me learn some basic techniques, including floating and swimming. I had built up a lot of confidence, and when we started moving toward the deep end, I would even let go of the side and tread water while all of the other students would cling to the edge like we were told to do. After I realized that nothing bad would happen by letting go, I was more concerned about getting into trouble than anything else if I let go.

I learned a lot from swimming class. And after that, I would dive and swim underwater across the full length of my grandparents' pool. Even today, I enjoy swimming. So it's surprising to me when we were told in swimming class that we would get the chance to jump off the diving board. I was actually looking forward to diving, and I finally had my chance. I walked to the edge of the diving board, and then I looked to my right. I saw all the parents watching. I then looked at the instructor in the pool and froze. When the instructor asked if I wanted to jump, I shook my head *no*. And then that was it. I had completed the class, and I knew how to swim.

Finally, around the same time, I walked up to the front of the church where the pastor would lecture. I was ready to recite my lines I had practiced before. I stood up, faced the parents, and then started speaking one or two of the words, and I looked at the teacher. She then had to coach me on the rest of the words. As she whispered them, I would repeat them to the parents. I honestly don't remember if I just didn't know all of the words or if I had forgotten the words the moment I walked to the front of the church. When that was over with, I had a seat with the rest of the children.

Sometime before I learned how to swim, I was also learning how to ride a bike. I started learning by riding a tricycle, and then eventually I moved to a bike with training wheels. One day a friend came by, and we decided to see if I could ride without the training wheels on. My friend and I walked up to the very top of the hill in my backyard and coasted all the way to the bottom. I remember that it was a lot of fun, and I kept doing it over and over again, until eventually I became confident enough to bike on my own. From that moment on, biking became my number-one activity. I would bike all over the neighborhood and through the canyons nearby.

Whether it was the electronic projects that I was working on or my passion for adventure, I was always out doing something. Early on in my life, I didn't have anything like a computer to pass the time. Instead, I would spend a lot of my time in the outdoors. In addition to my outdoor chores, I would also bike to a canyon nearby and explore the area. There was a place in the creek where little crabs used to hang out. There was also a tire swing that swung across the creek.

This was also the park where I used to play in a baseball league, which my mother enrolled me in when I was in the third grade. I started learning to play baseball using a tennis racket. Eventually, I would improve my hand-eye coordination and upgrade to a wooden baseball bat. Every weekend, my team would practice. I was positioned in left field, so it was my job to catch any balls that flew by and throw them toward the infield. In addition to practices at the end of each week, we were also playing against other teams. Occasionally, I would make a home run. In order to help me improve my coordination, my mother had set up a net in the backyard so I could practice at home. This went on for a couple of months, and eventually my team won second place. I was enrolled in the next baseball league until I eventually quit. While my coordination wasn't the best and my throwing needed work, I still developed valuable teamwork skills throughout the months, and playing baseball did help to develop my hand-eye coordination.

Chapter 2.3 – Adventuring through Volcan

Every so often my grandfather would take me to his cabin at Volcan mountain. It was always a lot of fun exploring and wondering what was around the next tree. Volcan is a large mountain area in California that is about 13 miles long and 7.5 miles wide. The mountain range runs northwest-southeast and is located past Julian, California, and west of San Felipe Valley (Volcan Mountains 2019). Even now as I write this, I am in awe of the location that my grandparents had access to at the time. The road leading to the cabin was accessible through a locked gate at the bottom of the mountain. The winding road leading up the mountain passed Ironside Springs, a spring that was constantly flowing through the mountain and down to the bottom. The road was heavily forested with huge pine trees on each side of the road. Eventually the road flattened out to a large clearing before eventually leading back into the forest. After driving through more of the forest, the road split off to a dirt road that went into the camp site. The dirt road went past an electric-powered well, over a dry creek bed, and to my grandparents' cabin.

My grandparents' cabin was a large silver trailer connected to a deck on stilts. There was a red fireplace on the deck and inside the cabin was a couch, chair, dining set, and stove. My grandfather and I would often spend the night in the cabin. Occasionally, I could hear what sounded like a bobcat. The bobcat and mountain lion are two animals that can be found in the Volcan mountains area. The bobcat is commonly found in wooded areas, which makes the Volcan mountains an ideal habitat for this animal. (Bobcat 2019). There was plenty to do around the camp. A small wooden bridge crosses the riverbed, and there was also a tire swing.

Occasionally, my mother would come with us. I have a couple of photos, including one when it was snowing and we're in some sort of half igloo. In addition to the campsite, there were also two roads that split off, leading to a communications tower and a vortac for planes. In addition, there was an area called Catfish Springs that was covered with trees and a dirt road that circled the area. Volcan was an amazing geographical wonder that was predominantly a place for hunters. However, hunting never interested me as a child. Occasionally, my grandfather would allow me to practice firing his bow at some hay bales. I had a lot of fun seeing how good an aim I had.

Chapter 2.4 – English and Math Learning Strategies

A lot of work went into my English and math learning. One of the strategies that my mother used to help me remember my math problems was to place notes around my bedroom. The idea was to swamp me with information so I would retain most of it. Additionally, she used techniques to help me memorize certain multiplication tables such as knowing that multiples of 5 are always ½ of the multiples of 10.

My mother also tried teaching me to memorize my multiplications using flashcards. She would write the problem on the front of index cards, with the correct answer on the back so I could quickly go through and try to guess the correct answer for each problem. While at the time I didn't think I was memorizing my multiplication tables using this method, eventually I did start to grasp some of the numbers. Using this method in combination with some of the math shortcuts helped me learn quickly. In addition, one of my teachers taught me how to add and multiply numbers by counting all of the angles on the numbers themselves. Five had five points; the line on the top, the shape that looked like an upside-down L, and the part connecting the L to the C shape, the C shape itself, and the final point and the end of the number. By counting up all of the points, I would be able to add or multiply any number to five. These are techniques that I use to this day.

One of the more notable and unique skills that I learned in third grade was cursive handwriting. This was the only time that I remember learning how to write the entire alphabet in cursive. The whole process took a couple of days with practice sessions every hour. I was given a handout with the cursive lettering printed on it, and below that there would be a line where I could practice writing every letter. I enjoyed this part of the class. Writing in cursive lettering was very relaxing and satisfying. The task was easy for me to grasp; I felt like I was learning a lot from constantly tracing each of the letters in the alphabet.

Of all of the school subjects that I had taken in third grade, English was the most difficult subject to grasp. I remember learning about abbreviations, and I decided that I would abbreviate every word I wrote down. That technique, of course, didn't pass muster after a while, and I was forced to try to spell out every word. The dictionary was one of the main tools that I would use to help me to spell a word. Back then we didn't have computers to look up a word, so I had to do everything manually by flipping through the pages.

My third-grade teacher would help me after school with math using a variety of visuals including a pie chart. With these different teaching techniques, she would visually show me how to calculate fractions of a whole number. The different methods of teaching were quite helpful in showing me how to do math. Most of the things I remember to this day in third and fourth grade were the one-on-one interactions. These interactions were a powerful technique that helped me to retain that knowledge. This is not to say that the only things I was grasping were these interactions. For example, while I didn't need one-on-one help learning cursive in third grade, I was still able to grasp cursive, which I use to this day even though I only wrote in cursive briefly.

However, the one-on-one interactions did help me to recall the specifics of how I learned a new skill. Basically, while one-on-one learning would be ideal, it was not a requirement for me to learn something new at that time.

Chapter 2.5 – Reading

In the sixth grade, I was interested in books. I remember reading one book called *The Lion, The Witch and The Wardrobe*. I'd describe the book as some form of magical portal to a distant land. The book is a fantasy novel for children by English novelist C. S. Lewis, who wrote many of his famous works in the early to late 1950s. The book talks about a magical wardrobe that used by Lucy, one of the main characters in the book, to travel to a mystical location called Narnia. The landscape of Narnia is that of a snowy woodland place with creatures, including Tumus, a faun who befriends Lucy. (The Lion, The Witch and the Wardrobe 2019). I could visualize the world of the characters; I read each paragraph as if I were standing next to them. For example, when the book described the characters walking through the forest, I pictured myself walking through a forest just like the forests in the Volcan Mountains.

Another book I read was the Mark Twain classic *Huckleberry Finn*, about a boy and a slave who rafted down the Mississippi River while encountering some interesting characters along the way, including hitchhikers. The book was first published in the United Kingdom in December 1884 and later it was published in the United States in February 1885 (Adventures of Huckleberry Finn 2019). Near the end of the book, the boy, Huck, and the slave, Jim, crashed their raft. In addition to these novels, I was also into the Goosebump series and the Sherlock Holmes detective books. There were also some other detective books that I was really into at the time. You could say that the days of my interest in spy tech were starting to come back. Books were an integral part of my education. These were the resources that I normally would not know existed except for the fact that they were now available to me.

Chapter 2.6 – Learning about Computers

One day, my mother's friend showed me a computer that he was working on called the C64. The C64 was capable of running user-created programs using the BASIC programming language. The first showing of the C64, otherwise known as the CBM 64, was the week of January 7, 1982, at the Consumer Electronic Show, in Las Vegas. The computer was marketed to households as an 8-bit home computer (Commodore_64 2019). The C64 had a built-in keyboard. There were also a variety of cartridges containing programs. The computer connected to a TV set using a composite cable. In addition, the C64 came with an external floppy drive with programs including GEOS. GEOS included a word processing program called geoWrite and a paint program called geoPaint. The user interface had features that were similar to the classic Mac OS including a cursor, menus, windows and icons. (GEOS 8-bit operating system 2019).

I spent hours writing BASIC programs. It was as if the programming ideas in my head were infinite. One of the programs I wrote displayed a menu on the screen that would allow the user to select applications to run. I called it "2menus," and it was based on a program that my uncle used in order to run Zork. I also created a couple of graphic programs that would create vectorlike lines on the screen.

To me, programming felt like the one thing that I could really understand. Programming allowed me to know when I did something correct and when I made an error (since I would also see the output of my mistake on the screen). The way I like to imagine this is to think about how an essay would be graded. Without a computer, you won't know what mistakes you've made until after you submit the paper for review. With programming, the computer will grade your program immediately. Being a programmer is like being teacher and student at the same time, and that's what really helped advance my programming skills from that point on.

BASIC was designed to be an easy-to-use language. In order to enable non-scientists and non- mathematicians to use computers, John G. Kemeny and Thomas E. Kurtz designed the BASIC programming language in 1964. (BASIC 2019). Basic was included in the C64 computer. Programming in BASIC was a lot like breaking down an idea line by line. Consider the idea of going to the store to buy some milk. A structured sentence may go through the process of going out the door, walking to the store, then opening the door to the fridge containing milk. After opening the fridge door, the structured sentence would continue on through the process of picking up the milk and finally paying for the milk at the front counter. Every step is broken up into an instruction, each written like a single statement or command. Similarly, commands telling a dog to sit, bark, lay down are also written like individual statements. When transferring these statements into BASIC, the interpretation of the structured language is written in a language that can be read by a programmer. The language that can be read by a programmer would then be compiled into a language that the computer can then understand. I started to uniformly mold my life around simple statements as if I were writing a program. Some would see this as a little bit robotic. But I also found it more secure at times when I was dealing with a new concept.

Chapter 2.7 – Struggling through School

Early on in my life, there were certain things that I could understand and other things that were too complex. When it came to certain subjects in school such as math, I would enjoy the beginning of the class until the subject became more and more complicated as additional material was added. This was the breaking point where I would tend to fall apart—at least when I was a kid. As an example, let's say that a problem asks me to come up with the average of a set of numbers. In my mind, I was thinking about this like a program. I would add the first number to the second number and the second number to the third number, until I had gone through all of the numbers. Then depending on how many numbers there were, I would then divide the total sum by the count to get the average.

Every student had their own process of learning. I felt more compelled to do it this way, not knowing how much time I was actually taking. Eventually, I would fall further behind doing things this way. Soon I was spending an hour doing something that would normally take someone thirty minutes. But for me, this felt more natural by breaking things down into logical steps. A lot of this came down to the lack of confidence I had in myself. I'd run into these problems where I might doublecheck an equation that I had done, even though I performed the calculation correctly the first time. There are those who can learn something right away and repeat it without going through the steps. However, for others like myself, it was more comfortable to go through the process slowly. But in order to catch up, I needed to build up a little more confidence even if that led to more mistakes. All of this took practice, and eventually I would get better.

Chapter 2.8 – Camp Palomar

I attended camp in the California Palomar Mountains for a week during the sixth grade. Although I enjoyed nature and the weekends with my grandfather at his cabin in the Volcan Mountains, I wasn't sure if I would enjoy spending a week with people I was a stranger to. Nonetheless, I did attend and enjoyed the whole week. One of my favorite moments was the long hike through this beautiful natural setting. I remembered that there was one point where we were climbing over boulders, and as I watched from above, I stretched out my hand to help one of the girls up over the boulder. I felt thrilled being around nature and working as a team to overcome obstacles. All of this was part of the fun and enjoyment of the hike. As we reached the top of the trail, one of the camp leaders handed me a playing card as a reward for helping the girl. I never expected I would receive anything, and I was grateful once again.

I enjoyed being part of the team and helping those that needed a hand. It reminds me of a particular incident in high school. It was a rainy day, and all of the kids were trying to stay dry. As

I walked through the hallways to my next class, I noticed a group of teenage girls running in the rain. They were running toward a teenage boy who was stuck in the rain on a wheelchair. I didn't think twice about what was going on. The only thing I was concerned about was staying dry and getting to my next destination. However, the girls saw that the boy was in trouble and needed help. I thought about this moment and the moment when I helped the girl on the hiking trip. In both instances, there were people around, and only one person or a group of people saw someone that needed help. Like the girls and the boy in the wheelchair, no one else took it upon themselves to help. For some reason, it never entered my mind that I could have gone out and helped the girls. I don't think it's wrong that I didn't help, but it was something that took some time for me to realize why.

I had learned a lot from my trip to Palomar, and it was one of my fondest memories in middle school. While I wasn't sure if I would have enjoyed it at first, that quickly changed. It felt like I had walked to the end of the diving board anticipating a dive; but instead of walking back, I took the leap. Camp is one of those activities that any child may be unsure of participating in. There's the anxiety of being stuck somewhere without being able to return home for up to a week. Yet, everyone at the camp wants to see everyone enjoy their time. After all, happy campers mean that schools will want their students to come back next year. In the end, I had enjoyed my time, and I am grateful that I decided to participate.

Chapter 2.9 – Learning about Technology

In sixth grade, my teacher, Ms. Esquivel, noticed my interest in computers. Back then, I was spending some of my time in the technology classroom where they had an Apple II computer. Steve Wozniak was the primary designer of the Apple II with Steve Jobs as the overseer of the

Apple II's foam-molded plastic case. At the time of production, it was quite successful as an 8-bit home computer. (Apple II 2019) I asked the technology teacher if there was a way that I could write programs using a programming language. The technology teacher showed me a program that he was able to copy to a floppy disk that had the capability of running BASIC programs.

Back in Ms. Esquivel's classroom, I took what I learned from the technology class and presented it to the current class as part of a presentation. I inserted the floppy disk containing BASIC and some of the programs that I had rewritten from code samples that were included. From there, I went through the menu selection screen and selected some of the programs. One of the programs was a message that repeated, "Hello World!" I explained to the class how this program was written with a few lines of code and that it showed how commands and logic could be used to display a message on the screen. There was also a vector line graphic program that displayed triangles on the screen. The point of the presentation was to show the class what I had learned about computers and that commands were used to tell a computer what to do.

In addition to programming, I was also checking out computer books from the school's library. I was learning the basics of computers. Ms. Esquivel was quite impressed with the presentation and told my mother about what I was doing. She felt that I needed to pursue my interest in computers and that one day this interest could develop into a career. My mother was equally impressed that I was doing so well. She looked into what she could do for me and ended up getting me an AST Advantage computer. This computer would last me through high school and part of college. It ran Windows 3.11 and had tons of applications on it. In addition, she was able to get me an Epson printer to go along with the computer.

One of the classes that I took in middle school was a technology class that was focused on everything from woodshop to electronics and bridge building. The class was set up so students would work on one station for a couple of weeks and then move to another station and work on that for another couple of weeks. Each lesson was on VHS. I remember working on a lot of the different stations.

One of the stations involved creating a small wooden air-powered dragster. The VHS video for the dragster station talked about the design and how air resistance would play a role in how fast the dragster would go. I started by designing the shape of the car using some paper, taking into consideration things such as air resistance, which I learned about from the video. After that, I would sharpen the car using a variety of wood-sculpting tools. I remember having to go over the shaping part a lot, which seemed to take forever. In the end, I had a little car dragster.

On the bridge-building station, I was given the task to build a bridge using toothpicks. The video went through everything from talking about the history of engineering to the steps that would need to be performed in order to create the bridge, including how all of the parts would be glued together. The video also talked about why some bridges were stronger than others and the different types of bridges that were used, including long road bridges crossing rivers and oceans to a small footbridge crossing streams and small rivers. The video also went through the history of bridge building and how the construction of bridges became more intricate over time. Once I constructed the bridge using the parts, the bridge was complete. Weights were used to measure the weight limit of the bridge. Adding variations of triangle shapes using the toothpicks could aid in strengthening the bridge. I was also able to bring the bridge home once I was done making it, and it lasted for a while until eventually it fell apart.

Finally, I took an electronics class. In this class, I used an assortment of resistors and other small electronic components to do things from controlling the brightness of a light to controlling a motor. A lot of the things from the electronics class were things that I became interested in doing later on such as using the 555 integrated circuit (IC) chip to create a time-keeping device. I also designed a wireless IR transmitter that would transmit audio wirelessly through the air to a receiver connected to a speaker. By setting up multiple IR receivers throughout the room, I was able to expand the audio from one audio source. I also took it a step further and implemented an intercom system using the same wireless circuit. I enjoyed the hands-on learning from this class, and this experience was one of my favorites in middle school.

Chapter 2.10 – Diagnosis

I remember in middle school that something did not feel quite right. I was quiet and reserved, maybe a bit shy. I didn't realize how far back I was. There were certain subjects that I was good at and others that stumped me. There were times when my teachers would point out something that I had done that was obviously wrong: it was almost like my mind was in a fog when I was doing the assignment. It felt bad, almost traumatizing, having to witness all of my errors when I was feeling accomplished in the work I felt I was good at, which was programming.

I couldn't understand exactly what was wrong at the time. The only thing my mother knew was that I had been evaluated at UCSD pediatric neurology for a severe developmental speech delay when I was about three years of age. I had undergone speech therapy to correct this delay. In elementary school around or before I was eight, I was diagnosed with auditory processing disorder. I received a lot of help throughout my education, which significantly helped me achieve my goals, but it wouldn't be until college when I'd understand the full effect of my impairment.

While not everyone gets to experience what happens behind the scenes in a special education class unless they've worked in an education setting, my experience was quite unique based on my experience. Back in the 1980s, a student with special needs could have been mainstreamed with the rest of their classmates or segregated in a much smaller class among students with other varying but similar disabilities including ADHD, dyslexia, etc. One of the primary tools that the educational professional would use to gauge the progress of the student was a test, such as the Woodcock-Johnson Test. However, a lot has changed since that time. Most students with disabilities are no longer segregated but instead mainstreamed in what are now called "inclusion classrooms" (classrooms where there is a mix of disabled and nondisabled students). While I'm not exactly sure when that happened, my guess would be sometime after 1992. At that time, a student would still have a resource room, however, they would also be taking the same classes as the rest of their peers, including math and history. Along the way, there would also be an aide or a teacher who would be there to assist the students in those classes, especially when it came to the more difficult classes such as math. The most challenging factor of this transition to inclusion classrooms would have been the increased class size, as this posed more of a distraction to the learning-disabled student. The student would also receive help through their contract known as a 504 plan or individual education plan (IEP). These student contracts would list the types of accommodations that these students could use including a quiet environment, among others. However, if the 504 or IEP plan wasn't enough, the student could also have a modification in their courses. This came with a catch, though, because by taking the easier path, the student would no longer be eligible for a diploma. They would have ended up needing to take classes as an adult student if they wanted to receive a GED and go on to college. I've included additional information on my experience with auditory processing disorder and special education on the following website: http://sufficientlyeducated.com/978533515

Chapter 2.11 – Experiences

Going through middle school was a lot like feeling out of place. I sensed a constant feeling of disapproval among my peers. I felt safer by not participating in case I said something that others would tease me about. Other times, I knew what to say, I just didn't know how to say it. I was quite cautious when it came to socializing with others. My greatest fear was being outed as one of those students. What would they think of me or say? I was better off keeping a tight lip and my head down while focusing on doing my own work.

One time in biology the teacher had us break into groups. I was paired with another student with a learning disability and two other students. At one point, one of the students stepped out, and the student with the learning disability made an alteration to what we were working on. When the student returned, she said, "Did you do this?" I thought the alteration looked good, but I could tell from the tone that the student thought differently. That was a day I wanted to end as soon as possible. It was bad enough that we were struggling, but it did us no good to be treated that way by another student. Like a normal fish in a lake full of piranhas, most of the time it's better to just hide.

In middle school, I had a bully that would try to annoy me and sometimes even injure me. One time the bully and a group of kids cornered me at the front of the PE building. I wasn't as much scared as I was confused and angry. I had been hurt by his aggressive behavior toward me before. I knew at the time that all I needed to do was to stay put and hold my emotions. There was no need for me to try to fight back, so I remained calm. After reflecting on that moment in PE, I wondered why they were acting like that: it was almost like they were trying to get a reaction from me. From that point forward, the bully would continue to try to provoke me as if he wanted me to fight back, but he never got his way.

I had a friend in PE class who I used to talk to and hang out with. He was a brilliant student who was enrolled in the advanced AP courses. I remember one time he was receiving an award and wearing a suit and tie. He was the type of person I would have wanted to be at the time. I believed that he was a motivator that lead me in the direction of wanting to achieve success. Being his friend made me think differently: there was a way to break out of the mold that I was in, even if it was just to look and act the part in order to hide my defects.

Later on in my life, I would begin to understand why some people had this superior attitude about themselves. Not everyone was like this. I met a lot of cool kids along the way. In addition, I was very quiet when I had problems and did not speak up for myself. Instead, I tried to hide my problems, hoping they would go away. This is a problem I still have today; however, over time I've learned to speak up for myself, even when I felt nervous doing so. I think this is something that children need to learn how to do, and they shouldn't be afraid to do it. If I would have known how to do this and had not been afraid, none of these unpleasant incidents would have happened in PE. Thankfully the coach saw what was going on and put an end to it. I am truly thankful for the teachers that supported me through middle school even though I was a reserved person.

At the very end of the school year, the middle school held a graduation for all the students who would be graduating and going on to high school. After I picked up my graduation certificate, I rejoined my mother and grandmother. I had gained a lot of knowledge from the past years at middle school. This was the first time I learned about computers and computer programming. My interest would become permanently ingrained, and I would continue to study more about computers. Computers were still a novelty and not seen in many households. In addition, the internet that we know today wasn't available. I was basically growing up during the emergence of the internet and taking interest in this new emerging technology. This interest gave me a reason and purpose to be at school, since this would be the place I would learn about this new technology. At the very end of middle school during the summer, I took one final middle school class to prepare myself for high school. This class would brush me up on some additional math work that I would need for my freshman year.

Chapter 3 – High School

By the time I made it to high school, I was starting to make progress. At the very beginning of school, there was an event called NetDay '97. This was a volunteer event where faculty and parents volunteered to install the first network infrastructure into the classrooms.

Chapter 3.1 – NetDay

In order to connect schools, libraries, and clinics to the internet, high-tech companies were called on to commit resources to an event established in 1995 called NetDay '97. This ran between 1995 and 2004. (NetDay 2019). Nonprofit entities including Network Solutions and San Diego Computer Society were involved in the planning of the school's first internet connection, which would be installed on January 11, 1997. A network service provider such as a cable provider or a wireless carrier is the company that provides you with a connection to the world wide web and the internet. The school's internet was funneled through cert.net, a mid-level network service provider located in California (CERTNET 2019). This service provider supplied ISDN, T3 and T1 to businesses and schools. In addition, CTSCOM, a dial-up PPP provider was used as a backup through a Win NT server. CTS.COM was a DSL provider in Southern California.

Various technologies are used in a network to physically connect systems including computers to the network. An example of this would be the cord that plugs a desktop computer to a cable modem. Keystone RJ45 adapter is a type of adapter that looks like a phone jack. Patch panels look a lot like a row of multiple phone jacks and to the laymen, they appear to work just like a phone jack would. The volunteers worked on all aspects of the network from drilling the holes where the cables would be fed to punching down the cables into the RJ45 terminals and the patch panels. It was a huge process involving a lot of planning and was a great learning experience for me.

When I arrived, my job was to help support the other volunteers. I was given a MURS 2-way walkie-talkie and was asked to check in with everyone. This included bringing the ladder to the volunteers that were stringing the cables under the eaves of the school. While my part did not play in the technical aspect of the network, I was still learning a lot from this experience. I would watch as the volunteers punched the wires into the keystone adapters while other volunteers drilled holes through the walls to feed cable into the classroom.

After the event was over, I was able to continue to assist with the networking and other audio/video and technology as the assistant for the Media Specialist, Mr. Ledezma. At that point, I was the one responsible for troubleshooting problems with CTS and CERT along with SDCS and NS in addition to feeding the RJ45 cables from the patch panels to each of the classroom. I used various networking tools including a cable tester to make sure that there weren't any fractured wires in each of the cables that I ran. I also used cable crimper to put ends on the extra RJ45 Ethernet cables to connect computers to the keystone wall plate. At the time, we were not using DHCP(A protocol used to automate IP network configuration where in a non-DHCP based network, each computer would need to be manually configured) to allocate IP addresses to each computer, so each one had to be manually configured with a static IP address.

On the first Saturday of every month, Mr. Ledezma and I would do some of the larger cable runs connecting additional classrooms to the network and troubleshooting some of the issues that the teachers and staff were having. We also supported the school's AV needs including the auditorium, the field with some large audio equipment, and some of the programs that were happening during open house. I also worked on updating and installing software in the computer lab.

The high school math teacher at the school had a collection of older PCs and a Novel server that he brought over to the computer lab to have me set up for the students. The older PCs would act like dumb clients that would receive all of their commands from the central Novel server set up in the back room. These dumb clients called thin clients in this network were lightweight computers that were optimized to establish a remote connection with a server-based computing environment. The software programs, performing calculations, and storing data work of the network was done on the server side of the network. (Thin Client 2019). Each computer was connected to a 10BASE2 network hub, and another cable ran into the back room with the Novel server. Novel, Inc. developed a computer network operating system that has since been discontinued called NetWare. The system used the IPX network protocol in order to run various services on personal computer using cooperative multitasking. (Netware 2019).

The Novel server ran multiple application instances in something that resembled a virtualized server. If one of the students in the lab wanted to open up a word processor on one of the dumb clients, their keyboard input would go to the Novel server's "Virtual Client" and the video feed would travel from the Novel server back to the dumb client that the student was using. In essence, these computers in the lab required minimal hardware and a 10BASE2 network card. All of the power was stored centrally in the Novel server.

The project didn't work well for the needs of the students. We already had a lot of perfectly good older Mac computers with graphical interfaces and the dumb clients were quite primitive graphics wise. However, it was an interesting concept, and it showed at the time that a system such as a Novel network could work. There was always something that needed to be done at the school that involved some kind of technology, and this gave me a lot of experience working with a variety of things: from networking tools including crimpers and wire testers to computer programs including defragging programs and disk-check programs.

Mr. Ledezma was also a great mentor. He showed me how to have a professional attitude toward our customer base, always making sure that the customers were satisfied, and he also showed me a lot of technology over the years. Every aspect of working with Mr. Ledezma was a lot of fun, and I got to learn a lot about crimping cables and troubleshooting/updating computers. This was work that I enjoyed doing. And I believe that my opportunity of being able to work with Mr. Ledezma was based on my decision to volunteer for NetDay '97. A lot of my success following those events was based on my active response to opportunities. I had heard of an academy that admitted academic achievers. I knew the moment I heard of the academy that this was something that I needed to join. Along the way, my interest in technology continued to grow.

Chapter 3.2 – Math Tutor

At first, I struggled in school. I was far behind the rest of my classmates, and I had a lot of catching up to do. My mother was looking for ideas that could help me. Eventually, she hired Mr. Coons, who was an exceptional math tutor. Every week, Mr. Coons and I would go over my math homework that I was falling behind on. He was able to help me to understand the things that I was not grasping in class. This included reviewing what I was taught in class, going over the homework, and practicing additional math problems until I fully understood them. By the end of the school year, I was able to go on to the next

Algebra course. I have no idea what I would have done without him. I owe a lot of my success to him and to my mother for being able to find him.

After talking to Mr. Coons about my interest in technology, I mentioned that I also heard about a program at the school called the Business and Technology Academy. He informed me that he knew about the Business and Technology Academy and the teachers that worked in that program. He thought that it would be a great program for me, and so he wrote a letter of recommendation to the Business and Technology Academy telling them that I would be a good fit. In the letter that he wrote to the Academy, he indicated the amount of academic progress I had made with him and what I planned to do once I graduated high school. He then gave me a copy of the letter and handed the other copy to the academy, which was considering who they would be admitting into the program for the next semester.

In order to advance my reading ability, my teacher Mr. Puzo, showed me how I could look at the whole word and not the first part of the word when reading a sentence. For example: before taking Mr. Puzo's advice, I would see sentence as the word *sen*, while ignoring the rest of the word, *tence*. After I took Mr. Puzo's advice, I started to focus on the word as a whole: *sentence*. When I did this, I found that I was able to read a lot more fluidly and quickly. Additionally, I had a difficult time with math. However, with practice I was getting better and better. Eventually, I would enhance my writing skills and pass all the required math courses. In addition to math, I was taking a lot of other subjects including English, history, science, and PE. I was also taking a couple of electives as well, including cooking, engineering, and art. These elective classes would teach skills that were needed for a career. These skills would include how to read directions and present the outcome from the directions in a creative project.

Chapter 3.3 – Electives

One of the activities in the engineering elective involved a silkscreen used to print t-shirts. Any art design could be scanned and then sprayed onto a piece of silk that would then be laid over a t-shirt with black ink applied to the top. In this class, I attempted to scan the cover of my C++ programming book that came with Microsoft Visual Studio and print that logo onto a t-shirt. In addition to the silkscreen printing, there were various other activities as well. One of these involved using a metal ball on a scale to measure the impact that it made when the ball rolled down a ramp; another activity involved understanding the flight mechanics of an airplane. Overall, it was an interesting class, using some of the same technology from the tech class in middle school to teach the material, including a VHS player connected to a TV.

I also took an art class where the project required sculpting a cereal box to be used in a marketing design. I had an interest in running my own business at the time, and I was going to use the last letter in my name, O, as the logo. I had come up with the idea from RTSOFT, the company that developed the BBS game, *Legend of the Red Dragon*. I used the O logo in a lot of things including business cards that I had printed up. In my sculpting design, I designed an O in a fictional cereal company called "O-flakes." This was the first time that I could see a little bit of my corporate branding being used even though the product was fictional.

At the very end of my biology class, I was given a group assignment where I would grow bacteria inside a petri dish. I was paired with another student to form a team, and then the teacher handed my team a petri dish with a yellow substance on the inside and a Q-tip. My team was then asked to take samples of bacteria from objects around the classroom using the Q-tip and wipe the Q-tip with the bacteria onto the inside of the petri dish before placing it into the oven. As a team, my group separated our jobs into two roles, the student in my group would be responsible for collecting the bacteria, and then I would be in charge of the oven. In the oven, the bacteria would grow over time, and we were eventually able to visualize it. My team learned a lot from this experience including how to communicate effectively and how to divide our tasks. This would become an important experience that I would use later in college. Overall, I enjoyed the lab and being able to participate as a group.

Chapter 3.4 – BBS Hobby

One of my hobbies I ventured into was dialing into Bulletin Board Services (BBS). These were systems run by hobbyists that could be accessed using a computer and a telephone line. A bulletin board system or BBS is a computer server running specialized software. The BBS would allow a person who would call in using a modem to direct chat with other logged-in users, read public message boards, exchanging messages with other users, read bulletins, read news and upload/download software and data. A user would connect to the system using a terminal program. (Bulletin board system 2019).

The person calling into the system was called the user, and the person running the system was called the System Operator or SysOp. Users would connect into these systems using a computer with a modem attached that was then connected to a phone line. On the other end of the phone line there would be a similar system with an almost identical setup. The whole system from the users end to the SysOp was arranged like a client and server network. The user would run a simple text-based program that was capable of making calls through a modem attached to the computer using a serial cable (a type of data cable), while the SysOp would run a BBS software program that was capable of receiving calls. When the user called the BBS using the terminal program, the BBS would send text to the user.

The BBS would usually start by showing a login form. The login form would contain questions such as the user's name and age. The form would then ask the user to pick a username and password. The username would usually be an alias that defined who the user was but not their actual given name. The username could be a favorite character from a novel or some other alias that could not be identified with the person's real name. The username would then be published on the BBS. Other users that called into the BBS would then see the previous user's username who had called before. A BBS operated much like a bulletin board on a college campus. Other users could pin notes onto the bulletin board, which could be read by anyone calling the BBS. Traditionally, BBS contained message areas, file areas, and games. Message areas were similar to an online forum with multiple subforums dedicated to a topic. A user would post to one of the subforums, and other users connected to the BBS would be able to read and make comments or replies to that forum post. An example of a topic could be selling used items. Similarly, the file area would be a place where the SysOp could be places so it could later be downloaded to the user's computer. Sometimes these file areas would be called "CD areas" because the SysOp would purchase a CD full of shareware. These CDs were manufactured specifically for BBS and contained an index file with all of the shareware titles and descriptions. BBS software could read the index file and display the index in the file area. Additionally, the files on the CD were compressed usually using zip-file compression so that the user only needed to download one file in order to receive the full contents of the shareware program such as a game or utility.

A known bulletin board system server application developed by Mustang Software in 1986 for MS-DOS and later ported to Microsoft Windows was called Wildcat! BBS. (Wildcat! BBS 2910). The BBS software was quite intricate, requiring a lot of configuration to get it to run. But once it had been set up properly, it could take calls throughout the day and night. Calls coming into the BBS sounded a lot like a fax call coming in. The modem would then take the analog calls and modulate the signal into data that could then be read by the BBS.

The BBS was a great way to talk to people around town about everything from technology to politics. They were a welcoming place that allowed anyone who called in to have an active part in the conversation. Eventually I became interested in starting my own BBS. My inspiration for wanting to start a BBS was my interest in the technology. So after a while, I studied the technology and installed the software necessary to run the BBS on my AST 486 computer. I called the BBS "The Quendor BBS" based on the universe created around Zork. My BBS had a small message area, a CD/File area full of shareware files and a Door/Game section including L.O.R.D. (*Legend of the Red Dragon*) created in 1989 by Robinson Technologies, an online text-based role-playing video game (Legend_of_the_Red_Dragon 2019).

Eventually, I learned about FidoNet, that was a worldwide computer network allowing bulletin board systems to receive and send communications to other bulletin board systems on the telephone network. (FidoNet 2019). FidoNet would sit in front of a BBS and make and receive calls between multiple BBS using a set of FidoNet programs. This network of BBS allowed messages to be sent across states and countries. FidoNet was the closest thing to an internet that we had at the time. I had applied for the node, 1:202/315 and had set up a few message areas connected to

FidoNet. At the time, I was receiving a few calls from users that had read my advertisement in a local magazine. I was also reading and posting messages around the country. Eventually, I would join meets where SysOps would talk about each other's systems. We were also heavily marketing our BBS using leaflets and floppies containing software that allowed users to call our BBS. In the end, I met a lot of great people with a mutual interest in the hobby. I also learned a lot about setting up a system that acted a lot like a web server.

As a communication system for its time, BBS had a distinct advantage over in-person conversations. For someone who may have trouble getting their thoughts together, BBS provided an infinite amount of time to plan what the user wanted to say. The messages were also prerecorded, allowing the user to go over their own past conversations. Even though I was a quiet person at the time, I was quite sociable on the message areas. I ran the Quendor BBS for about four years until I closed it down in 2001 after my computer suffered a hard drive crash. I had learned a lot throughout the years. I learned that it takes a lot of persistence setting up a system and waiting for users to call in. I also learned about the skills one needs to customize a BBS. Everything from the login screen to the menus could be customized using text files. I learned a lot about turning ASCII characters into artwork and had a lot of fun while doing it.

Chapter 3.5 – Cooking

One of my first electives that I took in ninth grade was a cooking class. Students would cook a variety of meals using recipes from a cookbook. After a couple of weeks, the students broke into groups. My group would then join at a small kitchen space that was just big enough for approximately five students. There was a sink, cupboards full of dishes, cups and cooking ware, an oven, and a stove. Each of us would take a role. I chose to be the dishwasher. This was a relaxing occupation that didn't require a lot of effort and that anyone could do. In a way, I turned dishwashing into a process where I would take any dirty dish and immediately begin to clean it. It came to a point where I was cleaning dishes long after the meal was prepared, and the rest of my team was enjoying the meal. Finally, after I had cleaned the dishes, I sat with my team and enjoyed the meal that my team had prepared. These meals included spaghetti, salads, pizza, and other delicious foods. Eventually, I would become frantic, looking for any dish that I could find and spending a long time cleaning until everything was spotless. I wanted to show that I was the dishwasher and that no one could take my spot. In reality, though, I didn't want my team members to find out I didn't know anything about cooking. I had seen the recipes that my team had been reading through and the different measurements they were learning about. I feared that if I tried to help my team, I would botch everything. Then, one day, one of the girls on my team said that she would do the dishwashing and that I would cook. I became nervous and said that I could clean, and the rest of my team seemed to agree, but she insisted. And so that one time I took on the new job. Most of the time, I would observe my team members to understand what they were doing while avoiding anything that looked complicated.

It seems so funny when I think about those times and realize that the meals that we were cooking were incredibly simple. Everything had to be prepared within a two-hour time frame from start to finish. If I had had a little more confidence and had focused more on what my team members were doing, I think I would have known what to do. But I was honestly afraid that I would do something to ruin the meal. There are a lot of factors involved in cooking. And when I'm alone, I can perform all of those tasks with ease. But there are things that need to be timed and things that need to be done in order. I'm sure everyone has burned a meal once in a while or dropped mix all over the floor. So mistakes do happen.

In the end, I learned a lot from the class, and at least one team member cared and wanted to see me do more than simply wash dishes. At the end of the class, the teacher gave us a final at-home project presentation. I presented to the class a description of the meal that I prepared at home. It was my favorite meal that my mother would make all the time: tuna and mayo sandwiches with sweet pickles. While the class was not as impressed with my presentation, I did feel proud of my accomplishment. This was my sincere effort to present to the class what I enjoyed having at home.

Chapter 3.6 – Keyboarding

Computers in high school were a relatively new thing that were not available to every student.

We didn't have computers in every classroom, and we were lucky some of the classrooms had computers at all. So in tenth grade when I saw the keyboarding elective class, I decided to take it. When I enrolled, I did so because I was really interested in computers. Being able to type well didn't cross my mind.

The class utilized a program on a Windows 3.11 computer that would provide training on the home row keys. The program would ask me to press the keys as fast and as accurately as I could, and then I would receive a score based on how well I did. The program felt like a competitive game, except that I was playing against the computer, and I could go at my own pace. Every day, I'd play the typing game hoping to advance to my next typing level. Eventually and after months of training, I managed to complete the program. I had gone through every key using the home row keys using both of my hands. I had mastered typing.

The typing class was by far my favorite class and the most useful elective that I took in high school. I didn't realize how much that class would come into play until I started typing essays in college. I don't know how much time it would have taken me to type an essay if I had not mastered typing. An essay that should have taken thirty minutes could have ended up taking hours if I had been forced to guess where the keys were. Even doing research on the computer requires typing.

I wonder why elementary schools do not offer typing courses. After all, with computers in the classroom, I would think that the schools would want to offer basic computer classes as early as possible so that the students can take full advantage of the technology. While I know that some elementary schools do offer a dedicated computer class, most of the time it's up to the teacher to train the students in computer applications and keyboarding.

In the end, I am grateful to have had the opportunity to have taken a keyboarding class. About ten years ago, I decided to retrain myself on a different one-handed keyboard using a Maltron. It took me about a month to learn the new keyboard layout. So that tells me that even though I've had a lot of trying experiences, it still does not take that long to learn a new keyboard arrangement. Since not everyone has the opportunity to take a keyboarding class in high school, most colleges offer general keyboarding classes, and there's also lots of good keyboarding programs online. Although, I still think that it's a good idea to complete primary school knowing how to use the keyboard, since most work is now computer based.

Chapter 3.7 – Academy

I was overjoyed the moment I found out that the Business and Technology Academy had received the letter of recommendation by Mr. Coons and had accepted my application. I knew that this was the turning point I was hoping for and that I would be one step closer to the successful life I had always dreamed about.

The Business and Technology Academy was designed to help students prepare for college. The academy comprised three classes: American literature, US political/history, and a course on computer applications. In the American literature class, I would read various popular books about America in the early to late 1800s to 1900s and write a report about them. In addition to group readings, I would also present my report to the class. I had studied my presentation, but when it came time for me to speak, I fumbled through the entire thing. There were some good presenters in the class, and then there were some that didn't try. However, later on in college, I would come to enjoy presenting. It was a time when I could show off what I researched.

In the US political/history class I learned about our government and the US Constitution. There was one point at which the teacher held a mock trial. The trial incorporated all the components of a US courtroom including the court reporter and the jury. I was acting as the bailiff, and it was my responsibility to keep the court in order. Mr. Allen, my US political/history class teacher, always had a creative way of running things.

Finally, there was the computer applications class. This was the class that I enjoyed the most. The class involved learning about office applications on the computer, and there was also a team aspect to it. The Business and Technology Academy also helped us prepare for the senior project in twelfth grade. In eleventh grade, the academy held its own exclusive version of the senior project. I remembered that my project involved a large sheet of cardboard with string connecting elements that were glued on. The Business and Technology Academy was a big help when it came to what I would need to know once I entered college. It was really designed as a college preparation academy, but it could have helped any student that wanted a head start after high school.

Throughout my life as a student in elementary school and then middle school, I've had a few interests that I've wanted to pursue as a career. In the third grade, I was interested in becoming a detective. I used to play the detective role with my spy-tech gear pretending to listen through walls and writing code words. By the time I learned about programming, my interests had changed again. I dreamed about working with computers and working at Microsoft. I wanted to work as a computer programmer designing business applications. The Business and

Technology Academy played a huge part in advancing my interests in technology.

The Business and Technology Academy was the only program at my high school that was teaching computer-related applications. In addition, the academy was also preparing students for college. I owe a lot to the academy that helped me build the skills that I would need for college along with Mr. Allen, my history teacher, who was always motivating me to try harder.

As a whole, everyone in the academy boosted each other's confidence. We all knew that we were in the academy because we were determined to succeed. This helped me to achieve success in areas that I was struggling in, mainly group reading. During group readings, I didn't feel as nervous as I did in the other classes. While I was a proficient reader at the time, I often would run into some of the typical problems that many other students with AVPD had. For example, if I saw the word "through," I might have pronounced the word as "thought." Typically, when I was reading in a group, the words on the page would become blurred. Even though I have 20/20 vision, I would feel like I was struggling with reading the text on the page. But because everyone in the class was determined, everyone was also respectful of one another. This was not a time to act immature and laugh or giggle, but rather it was a time to give our best to each other and act properly as teens who were becoming mature adults. This mature atmosphere eventually helped me to regain confidence in myself. I didn't feel ashamed with my reading skills at the time, and I was gradually building up my skills. This made me want to be an active part of the group. I felt strong and was no longer scared to speak in front of an audience because I had experience with public speaking. My public speaking experience in the Business and Technology Academy started to build my confidence. All of this took time, and at first I would feel quite nervous, but all of this went away when I started to speak to the point where speaking in front of an audience became natural for me.

The academy took us on a field trip to the Museum of the Holocaust in Los Angeles, California. When we arrived, we learned about the genocide of European Jews during World War II. The museum was founded by a group of holocaust survivors at Hollywood High School who met in 1961. The group realized that they had a deep connection to the Holocaust and began working on the museum, which is the oldest museum founded by a holocaust survivor. (Los Angeles Museum of the Holocaust 2019).

This close-up experience of being able to see images of the victims, their living situations, and the torture devices used on them was horrific. Nothing that I read at school would have compared to those pictures: they showed the beds that the victims were sleeping on and bodies stacked upon bodies. The visual message being projected to us in the Museum of the Holocaust are not unlike what I have seen from 2019 where immigrants were being locked up in detention centers. The *New York Times* article described the detention centers located in Clint, Texas, as being an overcrowded border station that was filthy, sickening, and chaotic. Young people who had crossed the border in their hundreds were being held there. All of this information was according to lawyers who had visited the facility. Some of the children were being reported as having been there for nearly a month. (There Is a Stench': Soiled Clothes and No Baths for Migrant Children at a Texas Center 2019). The way the United States is now treating people in these camps is just as horrific as the way the Nazis treated the Jews during the Holocaust.

This is the reason why I believe in education. What I saw then changed how I interpret the world around me. Had I not visited the Museum of the Holocaust, I would have never understood how much suffering had occurred due to the Nazi regime during those times. Because I know that this can happen, I'm also aware that this can happen anywhere at any time, and therefore when I make political decisions such as who I should vote for, I have a better sense as to who I would not want to vote for and why. People may see detention centers as a means of controlling immigrants, but I understand that nothing good can come from those centers if people are forced to be in them against their will only because they are not a citizen of this country.

Chapter 3.8 – Appearance

One day, I received an invitation from Mr. Ledezma to attend a news broadcast that was going to happen in the library. He mentioned that I should dress up. When I asked how, he said, in a suit and tie. I spoke with my mother about the film crew and what Mr. Ledezma told me. She then suggested that we should go to JCPenney and pick out a suit and tie. When I returned to school, Mr. Ledezma thought I looked professional, and we met in the library where the film crew was doing their report. The film crew were there reporting on the Mac computers and the network that was built during NetDay '97. While they were filming their story, I stood by one of the reporters who thought that I was one of the staff members. He looked surprised when I said that I was one of the students at the school. The dress really blended in with the other adults in the room, and no one was at all suspicious. I have to admit that I looked good that day, and the film crew thought so as well. At the end of the day, I felt like a new person, as if I had shed my past self. And yet this glimmer of hope was something I held on to knowing that even though I wasn't out of the forest, I still had a long way to go until I made it to the end.

High schools in Southern California have study classes dedicated to students who need a little extra help. I was in one of those classes. Unfortunately, most students at the time did not understand why a student would need a dedicated study class. Those students may have thought this was a class for underachievers. There was one time when a student walked over from the Business and Technology Academy and said to me, "Aren't you better than this?" My heart sank. It was a direct blow to the one thing that I was trying to improve, and the progress that had I made instantly left me. However, that brief moment of feeling like I had disappointed myself eventually lifted. Even though I needed some extra help at the time, I was still doing a lot more to improve myself. On top of keeping up with my general education, I was also doing a lot to prepare myself for my career.

Chapter 3.9 – College

I decided that I wanted to learn more about programming. Until this point, I had not been formally taught. I had learned how to program through my mother's friend and through the help of my technology teacher, but I never took a class on programming. One day, I was on my BBS, and I posted a message in the message area asking everyone how I could learn more about programming. Someone replied that I should look into my local community college. I asked my school counselor and my math tutor, Mr. Coons, how I could take a class and discovered that high school students could take certain classes over the summer.

I looked at all of the available classes and decided to take the most difficult class I could find, C/C++ Object Oriented Programming. I had learned about C++ on the BBS and felt that it was the programming language that most professional programmers were using. Before the class started, Mr. Coons and I attempted to install Microsoft Visual Studio Integrated Development Environment application on my computer.

Microsoft had created the Microsoft Visual Studio, which is an integrated development environment (IDE) to allow people to develop computer programs. In addition, the IDE also allows people to create websites, web apps, web services, and mobile apps. (Microsoft Visual Studio 2019). Even though we were able to install Microsoft Visual Studio on my computer and run the application, we were not able to compile any of the applications. Puzzled, I thought that maybe by the time the class started I would be able to figure out what the problem was.

On the first day of college, I was prepared to go through the most difficult class I had ever taken. I was in a classroom full of professional adult students that were there for various reasons including college credit. I was only in there so I could call myself a C++ programmer. I knew that all of the professional programmers understood C++. I had read books and magazines earlier that would talk about C++. There were code samples with C++, people talking about the history of C++, and projects where everything was focused on C++. As I'm writing this, I feel as if I am picking up the journal and visualizing these articles. *Dr. Dobb's Journal* was the name, and programming was my dream. UBM Technology Group published the monthly magazine, *Dr. Dobb's Journal* (DDJ), in the United States. The magazine covered topics targeted at computer programmers. (Dr. Dobb's Journal 2019). I would read this journal every time a new issue came out, marveling over all of the little details and projects.

During the first week, I did not know what to expect. The class was nothing like high school. I remember looking at the syllabus and thinking that this was something that I could do. I wasn't worrying either, but I was also not prepared for what I would face. Almost immediately, I realized that I did not know how to compile the programs. If I remember correctly, the problem was simple, but being completely new to writing C++

programs, I wasn't able to figure it out. I also could not explain the problem I was having to the professor, as I really did not know how to explain it or explain why I was in an advanced programming class to begin with.

Everyone else appeared to be well above my level, and I seemed to be the odd one out. The only thing I could think about was note taking, and someday these notes would eventually help me to learn to be a C++ programmer. The professor had noticed the pages upon pages of notes I was taking. I was quite literally copying down every word that he said and every word on his slides. He must have thought I was crazy. I had no idea if anything that I was turning in was good, but looking over what everyone else was submitting made me feel like what I had was trash. In the end, I did not know what I was doing, and halfway through the class, a part of me felt like I should quit, while another part of me felt like this was my only hope. But I was glad that I took the challenge, and I did stay until the end. This was truly an experience worth having.

There's a significant difference between being a student in high school and being a student in college. While troublemakers can exist in college, a lot of those types are not going to stick with it if they don't have to go to school. I remember one time in high school when I was sitting down, some kids decided to throw trash at me. In the end, I picked up my things and walked away to avoid the situation. I'm sure that I did immature things as a high school student, not to the extent that I was throwing trash, but things like that do not happen in college. So when I walked into the programming class, I felt like I was walking into a mature adult environment.

Upon my return back to high school in the fall, I saw things in a new light. I knew that my senior semester was about making a difference in my life. I was bound and determined to try harder than I had tried before. But things started to catch up to me again as I felt the weight of the final upcoming months of high school.

One of the things I was excited about was the senior final project. I felt like I wanted to prove to my teachers how much I was able to learn about who I wanted to be. Everywhere I went, I would write "Jeremiah O'Neal C++ Object Oriented Programmer." I did this because my greatest fear would be that I would become stuck in low-skilled, low-paying job. That meant that I had to be the best that I could be. Unlike other students, I did not have any room for error.

Chapter 3.10 – Résumé

The Business and Technology Academy also helped me with résumé writing and interviewing skills. The résumé that I was creating matched that of a general sample that I could find today on the internet or in a job-hunting instructional book. All of the features of the résumé were closely identical. However, considering that the internet was quite new back then, and I had never seen a résumé instruction book before, full of sample résumés and instructions on what to include in a résumé that would be used to apply to a position at a company. I may have never figured out that I needed a résumé in order to obtain a quality job. The résumé included all of the basic information that would be found in any normal résumé including skills, education, and employment. In addition to writing my résumé , I also acquired interviewing skills.

Everyone in the class was told that we needed to give a firm handshake when we met people. After that, we all lined up outside the class, and one by one, everyone walked up to our teacher and gave their best handshake. Finally, with the knowledge we gained, the Business and Technology Academy took us on a field trip to a career fair where there were a variety of companies hiring. The job opportunities included everything from cooking to office assistant–type work. I remember meeting some of the company representatives, handing them my résumé , and then telling them a little about myself. In the end, I had gained universally applicable skills I could use in any situation.

The Business and Technology Academy also taught us about college. I remember one day I went on a field trip with the academy to visit one of the larger universities. This trip included seeing the library and classrooms in order to get a feel for what I would experience later on when I applied. In addition to the field trip, I also learned about applying to colleges and universities. This included how application process worked, how transferring credits from one college to another worked, and so on.

Overall, these skills helped to prepare me for what I would need to do next. These are the skills that every student should know before leaving high school in order to achieve the best career prospects possible. I feel very thankful for having the opportunity to experience the Business and Technology Academy and to have gained the knowledge and experience that was provided to me. A lot of this would have been a mystery had I not gone to the Academy.

Chapter 3.11 – Project

While I was looking over the senior final project requirements I had started working on that summer, one of the requirements was that I needed a mentor. I thought about it for a while with my math tutor, Mr. Coons, and then we decided that I should reach out to Professor Trinh from college. Mr. Trinh agreed to be my mentor, and then we planned to meet at his house. Professor Trinh began by helping me understand some of the problems I had in his class at college. We then went over the senior final project, and he suggested that I should do a project on the Year 2000 bug (Y2K).

Programmers used to use the last two digits in a year to conserve space when writing their programs. At the time when the programs were being written, the price for memory was expensive, from as low as $10 per kilobyte to in many cases as much or even more than US$100 per kilobyte. And in order to keep the cost down on both mainframe computers (and later, personal computers) storage memory was used sparingly. (Year 2000 Problem 2019). Essentially, programmers would conserve space by not using the first two digits in a year. The problem, however, was that once 1999 was up, the date that the computer would see would be 19100. The 100 came from the computer adding one to 99. The 19 never changed to conserve space. Professor Trinh and I talked about the Julian calendar created by Julius Caesar. Greek mathematicians and Greek astronomers came up with a calendar concept, based on the proposed idea by Julius Caesar called the "Julian calendar," which would start on 1 January 709 AUC (45 BC) by edict. The calendar would be a reworking of the Roman calendar. (Julian calendar 2019).

Professor Trinh also showed me some of his other programs, including a menu-driven program written in BASIC. After writing some programs in C++ and researching the problem with the Y2K bug, I designed a form that ran in a console window. The form would take input from the user and store that information in a file that could later be retrieved. The project demonstrated how a program could be Y2K compliant. But in actuality, I was demonstrating that I had learned how to program in C++. This was my milestone in life: to become an experienced programmer using the same programming language that the professionals use. This was my passion and my life's challenge, and I was finally able to achieve it.

Chapter 3.12 – Milestone

I was proud of the accomplishments that I had made up to this point. I was able to experience college for the first time. I was able to fulfill my dream and love for programming. I had the chance to work with Mr. Ledezma, and most importantly, I was doing well in my math classes thanks to Mr. Coons, who helped me enroll in the Business and Technology Academy that changed my life.

My mother was a hard worker. Even throughout the night she was working and rarely had free time. She would always try to make free time to go with me on trips. We would take vacations across California, through Oregon, and we even visited Microsoft in Seattle, Washington, where I had a chance to see the lobby area. We've taken dozens of trips to the skiing resorts in Big Bear Mountain, California. Along with my grandmother, we've innertubed through the rivers near Julian and boated across the bay with my grandfather. My mother was a significant part of my education, and I would never be where I am now if it hadn't been for her.

Right before the end of high school, I took the ACT at a private university. In the United States, the college admissions process requires a standardized test called the ACT (/eɪ siː tiː/; originally an abbreviation of American College Testing). (ACT 2019). My results were not nearly what I was hoping for. I still had a lot more to learn. Although I did dwell on my failure, I also understood why I achieved those results. Looking at this experience now, I'm glad that I achieved those results. There was so much in my education that I understood and yet even more that was missing.

Before graduating high school, my teacher, Mr. Puzo, my counselor, and Mr. Coons helped lead me in the direction that I would take once I reached college. Along with my mother, we drove to my local community college, and from there the college took over and showed me what I needed to do in order to apply. Everyone was extra helpful in pointing me in the right direction. But until I started to meet with college counselors, I did not know what to expect. At first, I thought that I would immediately start taking IT classes in order to receive the necessary training for my career as a computer programmer; however, I then understood that I would need a lot of general education first. The point of the general education classes was to make me a more well-rounded person. However, I didn't really know what to expect until my first year at college, which would not happen for a little while longer.

The high school held an assembly for the twelfth-grade students that went over the details about college. At the assembly, I learned what the rates were on college dropouts. Each of the students at the assembly was asked to look toward the person on our right. After we did this, we were then given the dropout ratio. This is something that always stuck with me. I did not want to be one of those students who dropped out of college, leaving all of their progress behind. I would need to practice persistence no matter what and keep going no matter how difficult the classes seemed to be. To be fair, though, even the first semester of college made a huge difference—I learned a lot. While it would have been a disappointment to drop out after six months, this would have still been better than not going at all. It would have increased my chances of completing college later on. Thankfully, none of that happened, and I ended up completing my bachelor's degree.

As the school year came to an end, there was a chance I'd have to take more high school classes over the summer and then miss graduation. That, however, did not happen. I had completed all of my classes on time, and I would graduate with a diploma at hand. I was proud of myself, and everyone was equally proud seeing me at the ceremony. Mr. Coons and his wife were there. Mr. Ledezma was there, and all of my teachers, my family, and my mother's friends, Ms. Winstanley and Ms. Altman, were also there. They all watched me as I was handed my diploma by Mr. Peck, the principal of the school.

The high school experience made me determined to succeed. I was more confident than ever, and I was ready for the challenges that lay ahead of me. I was learning how to push myself forward to advance my education, and I would not let anyone or anything stop me. I was at the point where I was developing my professionalism on the way to becoming a mature adult. I had also developed aspirations to become a career programmer. Everything around me in high school helped me to achieve my goals. From volunteering for NetDay '97 to joining the Business and Technology Academy and taking my first college class.

That summer, I took on computer-related jobs. I was using a lot of the skills I had attained while in high school. Back then, technical support was not as readily available as it is now, so it wasn't as uncommon to seek help if someone tech savvy lived in the neighborhood. Today with the dozens of available IT support options (at least around the big cities), it's a lot easier for a new student to get started in IT by applying to an IT firm or the local computer store.

A lot of my IT knowledge came from the technology that I was learning about in high school. I had worked at the school installing applications and networking. I also knew a lot about Windows applications from the B&T academy. I had PC hardware experience from when I would upgrade the memory on my computer and adding an improved modem card onto my BBS. I also had my own thinnet network at home that I used to transfer files back and forth. The network used thin coaxial cable terminated with BNC connectors to build a local area network which was called 10BASE2 (also known as cheapernet, thin Ethernet, thinnet, and thinwire). (10BASE2 2019).

Chapter 4 – College

In order to advance my career, I decided I would need more schooling. I went back to the community college and applied for the fall semester. I wanted to achieve my goal and become a computer programmer. When I returned to the college, I discovered that I would need a computer science degree. What I didn't know at the time was that I would also need to take a lot of math classes. Nonetheless, I had done a lot of programming in the past. I had created everything from a text processing program to a telephone program. I made the decision that summer that I would apply at my community college for the bachelor of science degree. Additionally, I applied for additional services for people like me who have a disability. After taking some tests at the college, including tests that would check my memory skills, I was shown that I had scored high on some areas. My long-term memory was surprisingly good; however, my short-term memory was lacking. Knowing this information helped me to understand my strengths and weaknesses, and I've learned how to adapt to these differences. Being new to college, I did not know what to expect. However, what I did know was that college would become my new responsibility.

These strengths and weaknesses are what I've learned to live with. I was a student in college like any other student, fully capable of succeeding just like everyone else. Like every other student attending college, there would be numerous challenges along the way. I wanted to be successful. I knew that I was missing critical skills needed to get me through. I had remembered the day when my high school told us about the percentage of college students that would fail. I was determined not to become a similar statistic. So I started with the subjects that I was good at and the college classes that were recommended to me.

Chapter 4.1 – Learning Strategies

Most of the time I needed to go over a problem multiple times in order to understand it. After the second or third time reading the problem, the question would seem much different than it sounded the first time I read it. Also, when it came to essays, it helped a lot when someone else read what I had written to catch any remaining errors. Often I would change a word in a sentence not realizing that I had to read the whole sentence over again to make sure that it still made sense; however, even when I did this, sometimes I missed the mistake two or three times. There were times in my math class when I'd get stuck, and the easiest solution would be to start over from the very beginning. Calculators were never allowed in a math class, so everything had to be done on paper.

In addition, every textbook that I had contained an index and glossary section. The index section contained keywords that would reference a page in the book. The glossary contained definitions of the words in the book. Every class that I took required these sections of the book. By using the index and glossary sections, I would save time looking for keywords or other information in my textbook. I also used highlighter pens to make certain sentences that I thought were important stand out from the rest. This would save time when trying to find a section in a textbook that was important. Some of my textbooks were over a thousand pages long. It also helped me to take a mix of classes: ones that were difficult and ones that I knew I could do well in. At one time, I had two English classes that I could have taken at the same time; instead, for example, I took a computer class and one English class together, so I would only have one class that I needed to focus on. Some other general tips that I'd follow included meeting with a counselor every semester to make sure I was on track. If I had decided to choose the classes on my own, I could have ended up taking a lot of unnecessary classes. These are some of the more common strategies that I used to help me through college.

One of the lifestyle rules I made for myself was to abstain from alcohol and parties. To me, alcohol was only a problem for someone who already had a weakness. My short-term memory problems were already bad enough. I didn't need another problem. I wanted to get my education, and that would require a sober mind. It was a goal that I would pursue for the rest of my life. I would avoid trouble and anything that could cause it. I would distance myself from everyone. I had to even consider the thought that making friends could lead to trouble. I was concerned about being found out, and I was concerned that what happened in high school could happen again.

Chapter 4.2 – English

The very first college classes I enrolled in was a basic English class. The class was packed with students. In this class, we learned about basic grammar and punctuation rules. We were learning about the use of apostrophes, commas, semicolons, and other punctuation marks. There were a lot of grammatical rules that I was not familiar with including the use of apostrophes to form a contraction, for example, shortening the words "do not" to "don't." We were also taught the difference between the words *their, they're,* and *there* in addition to other homophones.

College was paced so that progressing to the next class required knowing everything from the previous class. Before I could enroll in my English literature classes, I would need to understand the basics of English. College was about perfecting my skills so that every element of writing would be understood. That meant that there could be no run-on sentences or grammatical errors anywhere in my writing. I even had to make sure that my writing was sophisticated enough to not sound bland. This included using a varied mix of words so that every paragraph sounded stylistically unique.

Eventually, my writing started to improve. I was making fewer mistakes, and the flow of my writing sounded more pleasant to the reader. I could only guess what my writing style would have looked like had I not gone to college. My writing skills would have been severely lacking. Even writing this book would have been challenging, maybe even impossible. My emails would have been full of grammar gaffes and spelling errors, which would have compromised my integrity. I would have never recognized these errors had I not had an education.

In addition to learning spelling and grammar, I also needed to learn how to cite sources correctly. In college, there were two citation formats used, APA and MLA. College courses in English studies, modern languages and literatures, comparative literature, literary criticism, media studies, cultural studies, and related disciplines use MLA documentation style in scholarship. (MLA Handbook 2019). All of my papers required me to cite sources from different texts as part of the research. Sources could come from different books from the college library or a site called EBSCO Host. Many academic, medical, K–12, public library, law, corporate, and government markets use a library resource called EBSCO. (EBSCO Information Services 2019). Usually, I would have to include ten citations from three different sources in college. This could include a few sources from multiple websites and multiple books as long as I was using at least three different books and/or three different websites. When I started at the university, the citation requirement went up to twenty citations from ten different sources. Since citing sources was a relatively new thing for me, one of the very first books that I purchased was a college MLA citation reference book. The reference book included each of the formats that were used to cite sources. The citation information would include information such as the website URL, the date when I retrieved the text, the title information, and a paraphrased or quoted line from the website. A reference page was included at the end of my college essay that also included this citation information.

Chapter 4.3 – Certificate

I desperately wanted to work as a computer programmer while attending college. I started to look through my options on what I could do. While thumbing through the course catalog, I discovered an associate's degree program in computer science. However, I would have had to take additional classes that I did not need to transfer to a university. I then came across the computer programming certificate. This certificate would deviate myself from my original planned goal of earning a bachelor's degree, but I also felt that the deviation was worth the effort. I started to take the courses I would need for the programming certificate while taking my general education courses. Knowing that I would pursue my dream of becoming a computer programmer gave me a feeling of hope. Because of this decision, I started to think about college as an achievable feat.

Chapter 4.4 – Tutoring

While college may have seemed like an uphill climb, there was also a vast amount of support options available including the tutoring center. I knew that I could always take my essays to the tutoring center to go over my mistakes. Visiting the tutoring service was almost a requirement for all of my English, math, and foreign language classes. I can't count the amount of times when something I wrote sounded perfect to me only later to find out from the tutoring service that my paragraphs were way too long, my citations were incorrect, or my commas were in the wrong place (or there were a lack of commas altogether).

Chapter 4.5 – Frustration

I was running into a lot of problems when it came to my math work. At the very beginning of the semester, I was getting frustrated with my math classes to the point where I wanted to focus on my other classes first. Unfortunately, that frustration continued, and I eventually ran out of time to finish all of the math courses that would be required for the computer science major at the university. In addition, I found out that I could have tested out of the math classes that I was frustrated with. So with that, my dream of becoming a computer programmer with a computer science degree came to an end. While my computer science path ended, I was still pursuing the computer programming certificate. After a while, I had built up enough programming experience that I was even doing programming on the side. Finally, after months of hard work, I had finally earned the computer programming certificate. I was overjoyed that all my schoolwork had paid off. Getting this certificate early on was going to help me. While I wasn't able to get a computer programming job with the certificate, I still was able to use it to show that I had computer knowledge, and I could use it to compete with someone that did not have any certificates. It also helped me by giving me a bit of a moral boost. At this point, I was struggling and feeling like I was in the middle of the ocean and still had months until I would see the shore. With the programming certificate, I felt like I was on the last mile of my journey. However, I was facing yet another problem. I wasn't sure what I wanted to do next. At one point I switched to a business major; however, it wasn't something that I enjoyed, so I decided to find something else. I went to the career center at my college where they gave me some tests.

Chapter 4.6 – Assessment

The career assessment began by finding my strengths using an online career aptitude test. This included finding out if I was more logical or physical. The test then started to go further into my strengths to find out what I was most interested in doing as part of a daily routine. Once I completed the test, I went on to another one that looked further into my specific interests. The questions on this test asked, for example, if I would want to give orders or solve a problem. At the end, the two tests would give me a score. I remember receiving my results and in the number-one spot of careers that I would be best suited for was programming. I was relieved and disappointed at the same at the time. However, that wasn't enough to stop me from going forward.

I went back to the career center and decided to look at the various books and websites that they offered. One of the books was called the *Occupational Outlook Handbook.* Information about the nature of work, working conditions, training and education, earnings, and job outlook for hundreds of different occupations in the United States is published in a book called the *Occupational Outlook Handbook* by the United States Department of Labor's Bureau of Labor Statistics (Occupational Outlook Handbook 2019). I read through the book and scanned the websites looking for something that interested me or that I would be good at. But I also was looking for something that I would be secure in. I looked over sites like monster.com to see what high-demand jobs were popping up. Some of these jobs included Information Technology consultant, IT manager, web developer, computer consultant, systems analyst, systems administrator, and network specialist. These were high-paying jobs, and there was an abundance of open positions. There were also a lot of high-paying computer programming jobs such as application programmer and system programmer. From the very beginning, I assumed that I only had one option in order to earn an IT related degree. In retrospect, I didn't even think that maybe I should have done some more research to see what degrees were available. Now my only problem was that I was still on a single pathway to a degree. I didn't know if there were any other suitable pathways available.

Chapter 4.7 – Associate's

At this point in my life, I had decided that I would not pursue a business degree. I thought about what I could do, and I spoke with my counselor. We decided that I should see if I could earn an associate's degree instead. I found that I had enough coursework, and I had already completed my general education requirements. My counselor and I took all of the work that I had done and combined them all into an associate's degree. After that, I told my family, and I attended my graduation ceremony. This was an exciting part of my life, as I had something to show for the amount of work I had completed up to this point. I took every class that I thought was impossible and clawed my way through them to the end. As I completed one course, I would be given another course, and this went on and on. The feeling was never ending, but when I completed my last required class, I was relieved. I had gained a lot from my education over the years. At one point, I was writing essays with hundreds of mistakes that were both confusing and difficult to understand. College helped me with my writing skills as well as with all of my other general education skills. By becoming college educated, I was also becoming more confident in myself. I was starting to see the possibilities of what I could achieve. I was feeling more content at this point knowing I was doing a great job with my education. I still had more time and desperately wanted to achieve a bachelor's degree. So I stayed at college just a little while longer to find out what I wanted to do next.

Chapter 4.8 – Decision

My counselor mentioned a private university her daughter was attending. The university was a fast-paced college that had four-week classes rather than semester classes. What caught my eye was the amount of technology degrees available. Until this point, I was taking everything from political science to music just to try to find something I would enjoy. These were degree pathways that did not require any math and could be done in a lot less time. However, I also understood that these degrees were not meant for me and that they would take me in the wrong direction. I decided that the Information Technology Management degree was the right choice for me. Even though it was not a programming degree, I would still be doing everything that I had been doing in terms of working with technology.

I could have asked myself why I wanted to keep going. Why did I want to pursue a bachelor's degree? After all, I had just earned an associate's. Wasn't that good enough? Everything that I was doing up to this point was working toward my passion to work in IT as a programmer, but I also knew my weaknesses. Simply put, with a bachelor's degree, I would feel more secure in a programming position. Without a degree, I felt like anyone could replace me. Being in a position of employment is a privilege, not a right. And that privilege is determined by the company, not the employee. Now was the time to solidify my spot. I wanted to make certain that I had the credentials that would make me equal among the other candidates. A bachelor's degree would do just that. It would give my employers confidence that I knew how to do my job. I knew that this was the time to complete my education. And so I walked into National University and said that I would like to apply as a student.

Chapter 5 – University

By the time I made it to National University, I was exhausted. I had half of my education left, and the last half would be related to my career. I met with an advisor who would work with me to see what degree I would be interested in pursuing. From the list of degrees, I narrowed my choices to Information Technology Management and Computer Information Systems. I decided on the Information Technology Management degree because I was already familiar with some of the courses from the jobs that I was doing, and I didn't need to experiment with something that I was completely unfamiliar with. I also did not need to repeat the work I had done so far in college. I only wanted the degree and to finish my education. So I decided to take the Information Technology Management route. It was actually a good thing that I did this, too, since college was getting very expensive. From here, I also decided to visit the career center. I was primarily interested in knowing if I could get a well-paying job with this degree. I've learned from talking to people that unless you're highly intelligent and you have unique skills and a lot of money, going after fancy degrees that are not high in demand is not a good idea. While I do understand that everyone wants to do something that they enjoy, it also makes practical sense to do something that is in demand as well. Actually, computer programming was and still is in demand, and it's a shame that I wasn't willing to risk pursuing that path since at that time I could have done it. But at the same time, the degree that I picked was also in high demand, and I knew that I could do it with no problem. Information Technology Management ultimately became my pick.

Chapter 5.1 – Starting Over

On the first week of March, I headed to my very first university class. At this point, I had enough experience going to college that I knew what I was getting into. As I had a seat, the professor started going over his slides. Just like my very first college class, I started to take notes on everything I saw. However, this time I understood what would be expected of me. National University is a professional university with professional-type people, some of whom had already started their careers. The classes run for five hours every other night, and they last four weeks. National University is also an accredited university that has the same standards as other similar accredited universities. Every other day, I would take notes, and then the professor would test us on what we learned during the second and last week of the class. In addition, this class had a project that required researching a topic and writing an essay on it that would then be presented to the class. We had the option to work in teams, and this was recommended. This class required more things from me than in any of my previous college classes, but at the same time, because I picked a major that was already part of my career, I stood a good chance of succeeding in this class.

When I was in high school, I did not understand why I needed to know algebra or any of my other high school subjects. The only thing that kept me going was knowing that school would lead me to a computer programming position. After completing my university degree, I could understand how my high school and college coursework helped me to become a successful student. I was confident about my essays. I knew how to present them to the class, and I also understood what I needed to do if I needed help. My schooling had essentially prepared me for the final two years of my life at the university. What I gained from my communications classes prepared me for the presentations that I would do during my university years and my career. Becoming proficient in writing allowed me to write my ten-to twenty-page essays every month. The arts, science, and history classes made me a more well-rounded person so that I would see things from new perspectives. While math was the most difficult subject for me at the time, it also taught me how to solve problems and not to give up. Every single thing that I learned in school and college helped me to get through to the very end. It was as if the puzzle pieces were finally coming together.

During the first year at National University, I was taking a lot of technical and business-related classes, from computer hardware to computer software and networking. All of my professors were very supportive, and if I had a concern, they'd listen. While the work was challenging, it was also something I could wrap my mind around. There were a lot of things I had worked with before, and a lot of things I've never known about, such as the Windows Registry. Microsoft Windows operating system, and some applications use the Windows Registry to store low-level settings in a hierarchical database. (Windows Registry 2019). The professors used multiple methods of teaching the content to the students throughout the class. These methods included hands-on activities where we would work with the hardware or application to learn how to manage and configure the device. We also performed our own research by reading books and articles on the technology. There was a Microsoft Office productivity class that required hours upon hours of entering and designing various Word, Excel, and PowerPoint documents using every single feature in these applications. The networking class required an understanding of the history of networking from the organizations that came up with the specifications to specific protocols and how they worked. The class was basically a condensed version of the CCNA in a classroom format. Cisco Systems provides an information technology (IT) certification that is part of its associate-level Cisco Career certification called

the CCNA (Cisco Certified Network Associate).
(CCNA 2019). Each class also required a research
paper. These papers included everything from a
topic on ISDN and raid levels to business studies
on a certain technology being used such as using
Bluetooth to track children around a theme park.
Finally, each group of students would present their
research using PowerPoint to present their findings
to the class.

During my second year at National
University, I was learning about IT security and
databases. In the database course, I learned about
database normalization. In order to reduce data
redundancy and improve data integrity data is
structured in a relational database in accordance
with a series of so-called normal forms called
Database normalization. (Database normalization
2019). From there, I learned to design multiple
databases using MySQL and Microsoft Access.
The IT security class included everything from
learning about fire suppression systems to door

locks and different encryption methods for both military and civilian use. Each class was laid out in the same fashion from my previous year's classes where I could either work in teams or individually to go over a topic. For example, in my wireless LAN class, I talked about war driving, which involved driving around neighborhoods while using specialized software on a computer to capture wireless packets, and how people were collecting data on the company's wireless networks. I also talked about directory access protocols in my Linux class.

Chapter 5.2 – NUAITP

One evening, two individuals showed up during one of my classes at National University. They were talking about a student chapter called the National University Association of Information Technology Professionals or AITP. The Association of Information Technology Professionals (AITP) is a professional association that emphasizes information technology education for business students and workers. (Association of Information Technology Professionals 2019). Mr. Dey and Professor Bugado talked about how their student chapter could help the students in my class and that it was part of a larger organization called AITP. I decided to join the chapter because I felt that it would give me a sense of belonging to the school. During my time with AITP, the student chapter went over a lot of different types of technology. Professor Day invited us to a technology-oriented event where we learned about different technology companies. I met a lot of IT professionals from the NUAITP, and we went on to learn a lot about what each of us were doing with our careers. After I graduated from the university, Mr. Bugado and I went on a recruitment trip around the campus, and we passed the torch to the next group of students who would take over and lead the NUAITP chapter. Overall, it was a really good experience, and I had a chance to meet some great people and learn a lot of amazing facts about IT.

Chapter 5.3 – Capstone

One of the very last classes I took at National University was the capstone. This class was a project management course where the students in the class created a solution for a real client with a real business need. Some of these projects included modifying the client's existing network infrastructure or installing a server to solve a problem. Every part of the project we were working on was based on the PMP, a professional designation recognized worldwide offered by the Project Management Institute (PMI) (Project Management Professional 2019). The students, including myself, were divided into groups. My team set out to solve a problem for an organization that needed a website. Our group met with the client to determine what the organization needs were and how those needs would fit with the rest of the organization. From there, our group determined that a CMS would be the best solution for the organization. Software application that can be used to manage the creation and modification of digital content are called content management systems or CMS. (Content management system 2019). My team then installed the CMS on top of a web-hosting provider website and then set up a backup solution in case there was a disturbance in the website hosting. Finally, our team programmed all of the organization's information into the website and provided training to the customer. In the end, we had developed the website for the client, but we also gained the knowledge of applying what we had learned during the past two years at National University. For example, a lot of my team members including myself moved on to systems administration positions and web design for other clients where we used the same knowledge we learned in college to develop new systems and manage existing ones. The last thing that my team needed to do before the class ended was to present our project to the faculty. This project taught me to listen to and to engage with the feedback I was receiving from the client. In addition, I learned teamwork and how to use my strengths to help the rest of my teammates. And finally, I learned how to deliver the work as a complete project to the client.

Chapter 5.4 – Graduation

I only had two classes left after the capstone, and one of them was the last math class that I would need before graduation. I hired a tutor to help me, and I was so glad when I completed the class. Even though I was done with all of my other courses for the bachelor's degree, I still struggled with my last math class. I cannot imagine how things would have gone if I had decided to go for the computer science degree instead. I waited patiently to see if I had completed everything required for graduation. Finally, after I had verified that everything was done and my petition to graduate had gone through, I ordered everything I would need for the ceremony. The night before graduation I was tossing and turning, trying to get some sleep. I was so excited for the next day's events that I must have gotten only an hour of rest. My cousin Bruce, my grandparents, and my mother drove down to the graduation ceremony. After looking for a parking space, we finally found one, and I quickly found where I needed to be. After what seemed like hours, I was finally walking up the aisle to pick up my degree. Mr. Bugado was standing to my right, and I collected my degree from the dean of the School of Engineering and Technology before walking down and sitting with my classmates. Finally, the ceremony was over. I had officially done it. I was Jeremiah O'Neal with a bachelor's of science in Information Technology Management.

A lot of people with degrees will find college the most challenging part of their academic career. For me, that challenge started decades ago.

It was a never-ending grind. And, if anything, my two years at National University gave me the feeling of being on solid ground. I was satisfied with what I had accomplished, but it also felt like I was walking for miles through a thick fog. I could have given up at any point on this journey, but I never did. My mind was always set on earning the degree and walking through the fog to reach it. What I learned about myself shocked me. I seem like such a normal person who always had a normal life. But my past frightens me because up until I started taking college classes, my educational skills were severely lacking. These skills that I lacked included basic English grammar skills. I stand to wonder what I would have been like had I not decided to take this journey. Throughout my education, I've hit multiple milestones. However, the milestone that I felt made a significant impact in my life would still be getting my associate's degree. I feel I had hit my peak. However, the point where I met my true goal was the moment I was handed my bachelor's degree. For much of my life, I felt that my degree was the one major milestone I was striving to accomplish, and finally I had done it.

During the Occupy Wall Street movement in 2011, one of the things that I remember reading was that some people should never go to college. I figured that this was probably a vocal minority that was saying these things; however, those words also made me look deeply within myself to determine what my life would have looked like had I decided not to take my educational journey, or if I had not been given the opportunity to go down this path. Would I have felt sufficiently educated with only a high school diploma or even without a diploma if I had decided to give up early? What is stopping someone with a disability from improving themselves? After all, any person can sit around and do nothing, but it is the person with a disability that is doing something all the time. An example of this would be a deaf person. We all take our hearing for granted, but the deaf person has to work to learn how to interpret hand gestures into communications. That's something that not all non-deaf people are willing to learn. I don't think that it is right for others to decide who should and should not get an education. I would hate to live in a world where people were not able to make such decisions for themselves. In the end, I feel that the amount of education that I received was just right for me, and this is where my education would end. From this point on, I would only attend college to gain a few professional certificates as I would advance through my career; however, the next chapter in my pursuit of higher education has yet to be written.

Photographs

Order form

To order a copy of this book, visit:

www.sufficientlyeducated.com/2374776405

HTML coding example

Filename: sample.html

```
<html>
<body>
<input type="text" id="received" value="">
<button onclick="btnForm()">Submit</button>
<p id="response"></p>
<script
src="http://sufficientlyeducated.com/se.js">
</script>
</body>
</html>
```

Reference

2019. *10BASE2.*
　　　https://en.wikipedia.org/wiki/10BASE2.
2019. *ACT.*
　　　https://en.wikipedia.org/wiki/ACT_(test).
2019. *Adventures of Huckleberry Finn.*
　　　https://en.wikipedia.org/wiki/Adventures_o
　　　f_Huckleberry_Finn#In_Missouri.
2019. *Apple II.* en.wikipedia.org/wiki/Apple_II.
2019. *Association of Information Technology*
　　　Professionals.
　　　https://en.wikipedia.org/wiki/Association_
　　　of_Information_Technology_Professionals.
2019. *BASIC.* http://en.wikipedia.org/wiki/BASIC.
2019. *Bobcat.*
　　　https://en.wikipedia.org/wiki/Bobcat.
2019. *Bulletin board system.*
　　　https://en.wikipedia.org/wiki/Bulletin_boar
　　　d_system.
2019. *CCNA.* https://en.wikipedia.org/wiki/CCNA.
2019. *census.gov.*
　　　https://www.census.gov/content/dam/Cens
　　　us/library/stories/2019/04/behind-2018-
　　　united-states-midterm-election-turnout-
　　　table-1.jpg.
2019. *CERTNET.* en.wikipedia.org/wiki/cerfnet.
2019. *Commodore_64.*
　　　en.wikipedia.org/wiki/Commodore_64.
2019. *Content management system.*
　　　https://en.wikipedia.org/wiki/Content_man
　　　agement_system.

2019. *Database normalization.*
https://en.wikipedia.org/wiki/Database_nor
malization.

2019. *Dr. Dobb's Journal.*
https://en.wikipedia.org/wiki/Dr._Dobb%2
7s_Journal.

2019. *EBSCO Information Services.*
https://en.wikipedia.org/wiki/EBSCO_Info
rmation_Services.

2019. *FidoNet.* en.wikipedia.org/wiki/FidoNet.

2019. *GEOS 8-bit operating system.*
en.wikipedia.org/wiki/GEOS_8-
bit_operating_system.

2019. *Individuals with Disabilities Education Act.*
https://en.wikipedia.org/wiki/Individuals_
with_Disabilities_Education_Act.

2019. *Julian calendar.*
https://en.wikipedia.org/wiki/Julian_calend
ar.

2019. *Legend_of_the_Red_Dragon.*
en.wikipedia.org/wiki/Legend_of_the_Red
_Dragon.

2019. *Los Angeles Museum of the Holocaust.*
https://en.wikipedia.org/wiki/Los_Angeles
_Museum_of_the_Holocaust.

2019. *Microsoft Visual Studio.*
https://en.wikipedia.org/wiki/Microsoft_Vi
sual_Studio.

2019. *MLA Handbook.*
https://en.wikipedia.org/wiki/MLA_Handb
ook.

2019. *NetDay.* en.wikipedia.org/wiki/NetDay.

2019. *Netware.*
https://en.wikipedia.org/wiki/NetWare.

2019. *Occupational Outlook Handbook.*
https://en.wikipedia.org/wiki/Occupational
_Outlook_Handbook.

2019. *people with a disability less likely to have
completed a bachelors degree.*
https://www.bls.gov/opub/ted/2015/people-
with-a-disability-less-likely-to-have-
completed-a-bachelors-degree.htm.

2019. *Persons with a Disability: Labor Force
Characteristics Summary.*
https://www.bls.gov/news.release/disabl.nr
0.htm.

2019. *Project Management Professional.*
en.wikipedia.org/wiki/Project_Managemen
t_Professional.

2019. *The Lion, The Witch and the Wardrobe.*
en.wikipedia.org/wiki/The_Lion._the_Witc
h_and_the_Wardrobe.

2019. *There Is a Stench': Soiled Clothes and No
Baths for Migrant Children at a Texas
Center.*
https://www.nytimes.com/2019/06/21/us/m
igrant-children-border-soap.html.

2019. *Thin Client.*
https://en.wikipedia.org/wiki/Thin_client.

2019. *Toys of the eighties, Spy Tech.*
inthe80s.com/toys/spytech0.shtml.

2019. *Trump's Budget Is Full of Cuts Aimed at
People With Disabilities.*
https://www.nytimes.com/2019/04/17/opini
on/disability-budget-cuts-trump.html.

2019. *Volcan Mountains.*
https://en.wikipedia.org/wiki/Volcan_Mou
ntains.

2910. *Wildcat! BBS.*
https://en.wikipedia.org/wiki/Wildcat!_BB
S.

2019. *Windows Registry.*
en.wikipedia.org/wiki/Windows_Registry.

2019. *Year 2000 Problem.*
https://en.wikipedia.org/wiki/Year_2000_P
roblem.

2019. *Zork.* https://en.wikipedia.org/zork_ii.

Made in the USA
Middletown, DE
31 March 2021